UK PRICE
£4.25

LIVER POOL
FOOTBALL CLUB
Candy

THE OFFICIAL LIVERPOOL

1991 ANNUAL

STAN LIVERSEDGE

FOREWORD BY IAN RUSH

HAMLYN

CONTENTS

Photographic Acknowledgements

Front and back cover: AllSport/David Cannon

All photographs are by John Cocks except for the following: AllSport/Dan Smith endpaper, 17, 19, 32, 36, 39, 50, 59; AllSport 20-21, 39; AllSport/David Cannon 6-7, 33, 35; AllSport/Ben Radford 34, 36, 46; AllSport/Simon Bruty 61 top; Harry Ormesher 37 top; John Cocks/Liverpool Post & Echo 56, 57

Published in 1990
by the Hamlyn Publishing Group Limited
a division of the Octopus Publishing Group,
Michelin House, 81 Fulham Road, London SW3 6RB

ISBN 0 600 57027 4

Printed in Great Britain

BACK ON THE GOAL STANDARD – IAN RUSH

People often ask me if I still get the same 'buzz' from collecting winner's medals, having won so many in my years at Liverpool. They've got to be joking!

The League Championship medal I won last season is as cherished as anything in my collection. It takes a place of honour in my living-room cabinet . . . because it's tangible proof that Ian Rush is back on the old goal standard.

A lot of folk had begun to wonder if I would ever be quite the same player again, after the two previous seasons. I'd had a tough time in Italy with Juventus, a year ravaged by illness and injury.

Then my first season back with Liverpool was a difficult one. It was only towards the end of that campaign that I'd recovered totally from all the problems and reached something approaching full match fitness. Then, although I came on as substitute to score two goals in the FA Cup final win over Everton, we lost the League title.

And that set the whispering campaign growing ever louder. The newspapers began to question whether I had lost my former pace and sure touch in front of goal. They also began to wonder whether I was injury-prone and had perhaps lost my enthusiasm, as well as my goal-scoring instinct.

I was confident in my own mind that it was only a matter of time before I regained my top form. But knowing that so many questions were being asked made me all the more determined to find the right answers last season.

And I think I did. I felt I played better than I ever have before in my career. Maybe there were not quite as many goals from me as usual, but I believe I have become a better team player – one who provides the openings for others, as well as still maintaining a pretty good striking rate of my own.

In fact, it was a marvellous season all round for Liverpool, as we regained the First Division title by a handsome nine-point margin. And I'm sure that nobody would begrudge our right to be called the best team in England once again.

Our only disappointment came in the FA Cup, where we blew the semi-final against Crystal Palace. I guess most of the country was supporting them, but that didn't make defeat any easier to take!

My striking partner John Barnes had a magnificent season, scoring some goals so spectacular that they would have been greeted as world-class, had they been scored by an Italian or a Brazilian.

But for me, our player of the year had to be the captain, Alan Hansen. He had his own injury problems, but he overcame them to lead the side superbly. as ever a wonderfully calming influence on everybody.

It still amazes me how the Scots could ignore him in their World Cup plans. If there is a better defender in the First Division, then I don't know him.

Ian Rush

SWEET CHARITY

Below left: Ronnie Whelan's command in midfield meant that traffic was largely one-way as Liverpool gained revenge over Arsenal in the Charity Shield. Adams and O'Leary attempt to halt his progress.

This was where Liverpool came in, with the Wembley stage set for a repeat performance. In August, 1988, they had avenged their FA Cup final defeat by Wimbledon by beating the Dons in the Charity Shield pipe-opener to the new campaign; and in August, 1989, Liverpool had a date with Arsenal at Wembley.

This time, they were out to make amends for having lost the League championship to the Gunners in the final game of season 1988-89 . . . and they did just that, with Peter Beardsley emerging as the match-winner.

Ian Rush, fit after injury, gets in a shot at goal. Although he failed to score, Rush's mobility and opportunism promised well for the season.

Liverpool had a newcomer on view – defender Glenn Hysen, captain of Sweden's World Cup team, and he quickly showed that he could slot into the Liverpool way of doing things. For another Liverpool player, though, the start of the season posed the question as to how long he would remain at Anfield . . . and, indeed, striker John Aldridge was to be on the move to Spain within a matter of weeks, after having to settle for an onlooker's role, as he took his place on the substitutes' bench.

When Liverpool beat Wimbledon to claim the Charity Shield in 1988, Ronnie Whelan was their captain, in the absence of the injured Alan Hansen; but after having missed the best part of a season, Alan was back for the 1989 game with Arsenal and walked up to collect the Charity Shield at the end.

Still the team to beat

So Liverpool, with one trophy staying on the Anfield sideboard, were all geared up to contest the First Division championship race, not to mention the two domestic Cup competitions. And once again, it was generally acknowledged that they were indeed the team all the others had to beat. As for marksman Beardsley, this was the after-match verdict: 'Bobby Robson saw Beardsley at his liveliest, shooting the winner and not being far from a hat-trick.'

And Glenn Hysen? – not only did he collect a winner's medal on his debut in English football, but he made it a memorable occasion twice over, as he was named Man of the Match.

Below: **The Charity Shield and its winners. From left, back: Ablett (sub), McMahon, Staunton, Whelan, Molby (sub), Burrows, Rush, Grobbelaar, Barnes (behind), Aldridge (sub). Crouching: Beardsley (whose goal won the match), Venison, Nicol, Hansen and Hysen, the Swedish international bought in the summer from Fiorentina.**

AUGUST

A SOLID START

Liverpool had three Barclays League matches scheduled for August, and the first of these brought promoted Manchester City to Anfield. Not surprisingly, City regarded this fixture as a very real test of their ability to stay the pace in the top flight – and, while they had reason to be satisfied with a fighting performance, they returned home knowing they had finished on the wrong end of a 3-1 scoreline.

RESULTS

Football League, 19 August

Liverpool 3, *John Barnes* (penalty) *Peter Beardsley* *Steve Nicol*	Manchester City 1 *Andy Hinchcliffe*

Football League, 23 August

Aston Villa 1 *David Platt*	Liverpool 1 *John Barnes*

Football League, 26 August

Luton Town 0	Liverpool 0

League Position

	P.	W.	D.	L.	F.	A.	Pts.	Position
Liverpool	3	1	2	0	4	2	5	5th

Liverpool's first League marksman of the season was John Barnes, who scored from the penalty spot with the game only seven minutes old. City full-back Andy Hinchcliffe shook the Anfield faithful by rapping home an equaliser inside half an hour, but on the hour Peter Beardsley struck his second goal in successive matches, and with 60 seconds to go Steve Nicol gave the scoreline a more impressive appearance.

Shaping up

Liverpool's line-up was the shape of things to come, with Glenn Hysen at No. 2 (replacing the injured Gary Gillespie), David Burrows back at No. 3, Barry Venison at No. 8 and John Aldridge and Jan Molby on the bench. Hysen partnered Alan Hansen at the heart of the defence, with Venison playing at right-back and Burrows at left-back.

The same team did duty at Villa Park, where John Barnes scored the goal that earned a point, then it was on to Kenilworth Road and a scoreless draw against Luton Town, with Gary Gillespie in for Barry Venison, who replaced Danish-international Molby as the substitute wearing No. 14.

Left: Century-plus goal-scorer Peter Beardsley looked set to continue his winning ways for Liverpool right from the start of the season.

Below: Ian Rush (right) looks on as Beardsley puts Liverpool ahead at Anfield with a second-half goal that set the seal on early-season defeat for newly-promoted rivals, Manchester City.

SEPTEMBER

ON TOP FORM

Four victories from five matches gave September a glow, so far as Liverpool were concerned – and if there was general sadness at the departure of John Aldridge, the joy was unconfined as Liverpool slaughtered Crystal Palace at Anfield.

Rams rammed, Palace stormed

But first, the trip to the Baseball Ground, and the goals flowed from Liverpool, as Derby just couldn't cope with Scouser striking power. It was a Rush job five minutes into the second half, a Barnes spot-kick with eight minutes to go, and a Beardsley killer on the stroke of full time.

But as Crystal Palace, fresh from the Second Division, tried their luck at Anfield, Liverpool could have been forgiven for saying: 'You ain't seen nuthin' yet!' Palace 'keeper Perry Suckling and his team-mates were shell-shocked as Liverpool pumped nine goals into their net . . . and yet, remarkably, there wasn't one hat-trick marksman.

Out-Gunned: Glenn Hysen climbs above Rosario in an effort to break the deadlock at Anfield against Norwich but Gunn has the ball and the match ended scoreless.

Goal Rush: To score against Everton is always sweet, but two in two minutes is real joy even for Ian Rush. Ratcliffe goes to pick the ball out of his own net during Liverpool's 3-1 win at Goodison.

RESULTS

Football League, 9 September

Derby County 0	Liverpool 3
	Ian Rush
	John Barnes (penalty)
	Peter Beardsley

Football League, 12 September

Liverpool 9	Crystal Palace 0
Steve Nicol (2)	
Glenn Hysen	
Ian Rush	
Gary Gillespie	
Peter Beardsley	
John Barnes	
Steve McMahon	
John Aldridge (penalty)	

Football League, 16 September

Liverpool 0	Norwich City 0

Football League, 23 September

Everton 1	Liverpool 3
Mike Newell	*John Barnes*
	Ian Rush (2)

Littlewoods Cup, 19 September

Liverpool 5	Wigan Athletic 2
Ian Rush (2)	*Bryan Griffiths*
Glenn Hysen	*David Thompson*
Peter Beardsley	
John Barnes	

League Position

	P.	W.	D.	L.	F.	A.	Pts.	Position
Liverpool	7	4	3	0	19	3	15	1st

Toffee-men licked

After that nine-goal bonanza, an 0-0 result against Norwich was a bit of a let-down, and when Wigan Athletic arrived to do battle in the Littlewoods Cup, they sprang a shock by taking a 2-1 lead. But in the end, it was Liverpool 5, Wigan 2, as Ian Rush (2), John Barnes, Glenn Hysen and Peter Beardsley did the damage.

So Liverpool were set up for Everton at Goodison Park the following Saturday – but when £1M new-boy Mike Newell struck, the fans from the Anfield side of the city were muted.

Not for long, though . . . because after 32 minutes John Barnes was striking, to level the score; and then Ian Rush, so often the bogey-man for Everton, beat 'keeper Neville Southall twice in as many minutes, with an hour just gone. So the final scoreline read Everton 1, Liverpool 3.

One over the 8

Liverpool rewrote the record books as they slammed nine goals past hapless Crystal Palace without reply, to clock up their biggest-ever victory in First Division football.

The margin matched their all-time League victory, a 10-1 hiding they handed out to Rotherham Town, away back in 1896. . . . but that was Second Division fare, while the Palace massacre was top-of-the-table stuff in Division 1.

Palace were taken apart, starting with a Steve Nicol goal after eight minutes and carrying on with a Steve McMahon goal with quarter of an hour

Above: **Glenn Hysen triumphant after his first-ever goal for Liverpool, the eighth of the sensational nine-nil Anfield slaughter of 'Palace which also included goals from Red raiders, Peter Beardsley and Ian Rush (right)**

gone. Forty-four minutes, and Ian Rush was getting into the act as he struck his second goal in four days.

A Victory Parade

As for the rest, it was like a procession. . . . Gary Gillespie's diving header produced goal No. 4, Peter Beardsley rounded off a one-two with "Rushy" to score goal No. 5 after 63 minutes, then substitute John Aldridge won the biggest cheer of the night when, with his first touch of the ball, he despatched a penalty for goal No. 6.

Still the scoring hadn't finished: just inside 80 minutes, John Barnes scored from a free-kick a yard outside the penalty area, and eight minutes from time Glenn Hysen headed his first goal for Liverpool, to make the scoreline 8-0. Finally, with two minutes remaining, Steve Nicol ended the evening as he had begun it . . . by beating 'keeper Perry Suckling as he struck Liverpool's ninth goal of the game.

League Record

And that meant Liverpool had set another kind of record, too, because this was the first time in Football League history that eight different players had scored for one side in the same game. As for punch-drunk Palace, it really was a case of them having had one over the eight!

OCTOBER

For Liverpool, October was like the curate's egg – good in parts. It started well enough with substitute Steve Staunton hitting a hat-trick to sink Wigan Athletic without trace in the second leg of the Littlewoods Cup-tie, and it continued with a 2-1 victory at Wimbledon in the Barclays League, with Ronnie Whelan and Peter Beardsley the marksmen.

Defeat at the Dell

Liverpool's trip to Southampton for the next Barclays League match was confidently expected to produce some reward as well – but, instead of giving the 20,000 crowd at The Dell something to think about, Liverpool found themselves on the receiving end, for once. And not just once, come to that – but four times. The Saints stuck four goals past Bruce Grobbelaar, and the lone counter came from a Peter Beardsley penalty.

Considering that the next assignment was generally regarded as a tough one, Liverpool had to view their Littlewoods Cup-tie against Arsenal at Highbury as crucial to their reputation for being able to hit back when stung.

Manager Kenny Dalglish played a tactical game, with Peter Beardsley on the bench and a defensive line which included Jan Molby, Alex Watson, David Burrows, Gary Ablett and Barry Venison. The tactics looked like paying off, too, until Arsenal sent on Alan Smith, and it was his late goal which unlocked the Liverpool defence and settled the tie.

RESULTS

Football League, 14 October

Wimbledon 1 *Dennis Wise*	Liverpool 2 *Ronnie Whelan* *Peter Beardsley*

Football League, 21 October

Southampton 4 *Ray Wallace (2)* *Paul Rideout* *Matthew le Tissier*	Liverpool 1 *Peter Beardsley* (penalty)

Football League, 29 October

Liverpool 1 *John Barnes*	Tottenham Hotspur 0

Littlewoods Cup, 4 October

Wigan Athletic 0	Liverpool 3 *Steve Staunton (3)*

Littlewoods Cup, 25 October

Arsenal 1 *Alan Smith*	Liverpool 0

League Position

	P.	W.	D.	L.	F.	A.	Pts.	Position
Liverpool	10	6	3	1	23	8	21	1st

But Tottenham are toppled

In the next match Spurs certainly tried to live up to their blossoming reputation, but Liverpool showed they were prepared to match them in every department, and at the end of the day they had three precious points in the bag, thanks to that master-marksman, John Barnes. He broke clear of the Tottenham defence, leaving Pat van den Hauwe trailing, then rifled the ball past 'keeper Erik Thorstvedt.

A ROLLER-COASTER MONTH

Above: **a stunner from sub Steve Staunton, just one of a hat-trick of goals that sent Wigan Athletic reeling out of the Littlewoods Cup and Liverpool into the next round against Arsenal at Highbury.**

The Anfield roar lifts striker Ian Rush off his feet during the end-of-the-month victory over Tottenham Hotspur.

NOVEMBER

BLUES AS REDS SLIP

Three away games, two at home . . . that was Liverpool's fixture list for November. Coventry, the first item on the agenda, looked straightforward enough, but Cyrille Regis chose the game to demonstrate that he hadn't lost the knack of finding the net.

RESULTS

Football League, 4 November

Liverpool 0	Coventry City 1 *Cyrille Regis*

Football League, 11 November

Queen's Park Rangers 3 *Ian Wright* (2 – 1 penalty) *Mark Falco*	Liverpool 2 *John Barnes* (2 – 1 penalty)

Football League, 19 November

Millwall 1 *David Thompson*	Liverpool 2 *Ian Rush* *John Barnes*

Football League, 26 November

Liverpool 2 *John Barnes* *Steve McMahon*	Arsenal 1 *Alan Smith*

Football League, 29 November

Sheffield Wednesday 2 *David Hirst* *Dalian Atkinson*	Liverpool 0

League Position

	P.	W.	D.	L.	F.	A.	Pts.	Position
Liverpool	15	8	3	4	29	16	27	1st

Above: **Ronnie Whelan rises as if from a trap-door. Liverpool rose to the top with a Sunday televised 2-1 defeat of Arsenal.**

Left: **Trevor Peake of Coventry gets shirty with red menace Ian Rush as they compete for the ball.**

Rangers rampant

Liverpool's problems were compounded by a defeat in their next match against Queen's Park Rangers at Loftus Road, so all eyes were on Liverpool as they travelled back to London to beard Millwall in the Lions' Den.

Lions tamed, Gunners spiked, but Owls still hoot

The Londoners tried their hardest to overwhelm Liverpool early on, and they did cause a few scares. But in the end they had to admit defeat, even though they managed to beat Bruce Grobbelaar. Goals from John Barnes and Ian Rush tilted the match Liverpool's way and put them in good heart for another TV test the following Sunday – against Arsenal at Anfield.

Arsenal did score . . . but goals from Steve McMahon and John Barnes produced a 2-1 result which in no way flattered the men who wore Liverpool's colours. And they were top of the First Division, with a match still in hand.

That match was played just a few nights later at Hillsborough, the scene of the FA Cup semi-final tragedy the previous April. Liverpool never really got to grips with Wednesday. David Hirst shot the Owls into the lead, Dalian Atkinson scored a stunning goal, and that was that. Wednesday 2, Liverpool 0 . . . but the Anfield Reds still remained on top, although this was only by virtue of their superior goal difference.

RETURN TO

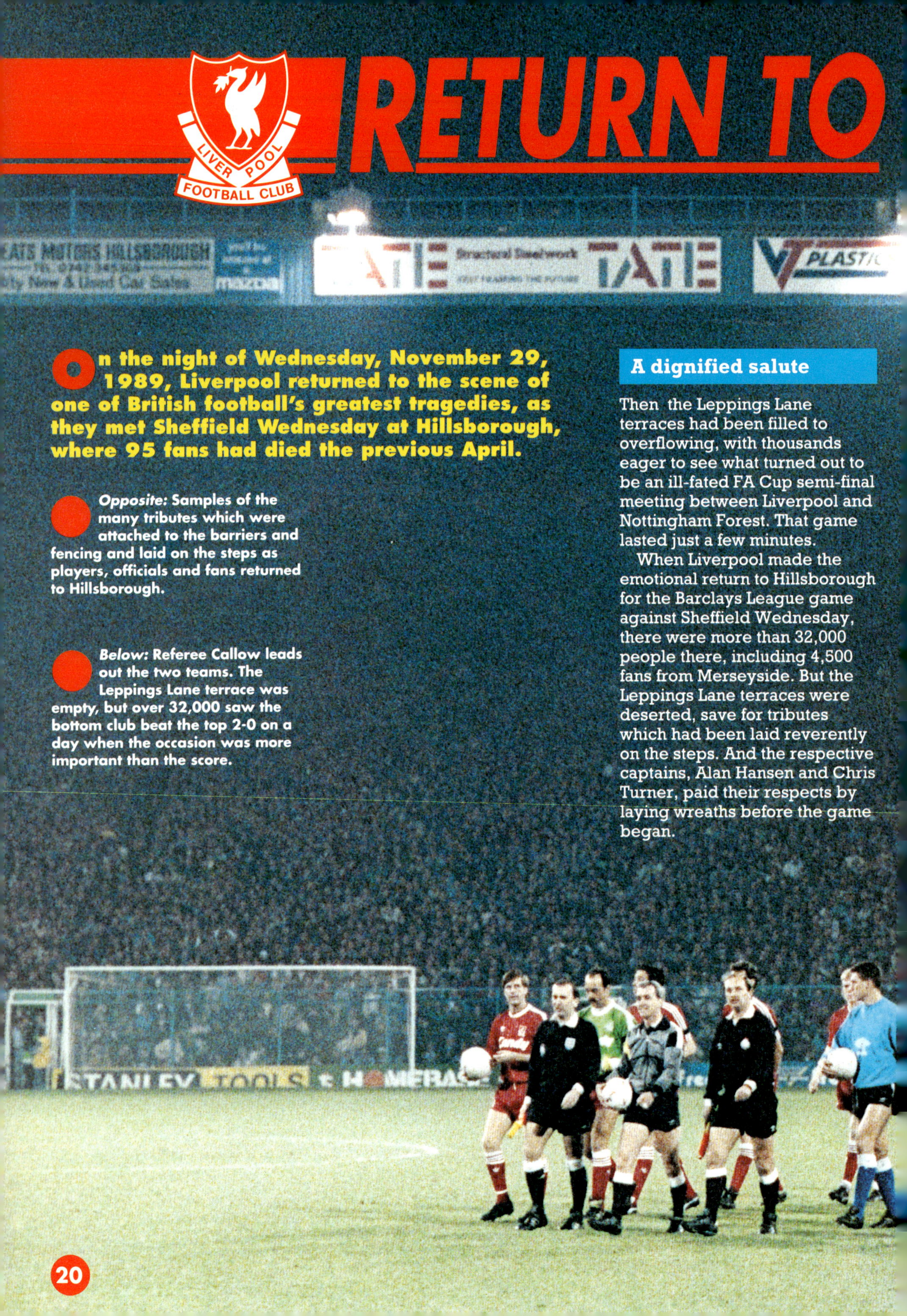

On the night of Wednesday, November 29, 1989, Liverpool returned to the scene of one of British football's greatest tragedies, as they met Sheffield Wednesday at Hillsborough, where 95 fans had died the previous April.

Opposite: **Samples of the many tributes which were attached to the barriers and fencing and laid on the steps as players, officials and fans returned to Hillsborough.**

Below: **Referee Callow leads out the two teams. The Leppings Lane terrace was empty, but over 32,000 saw the bottom club beat the top 2-0 on a day when the occasion was more important than the score.**

A dignified salute

Then the Leppings Lane terraces had been filled to overflowing, with thousands eager to see what turned out to be an ill-fated FA Cup semi-final meeting between Liverpool and Nottingham Forest. That game lasted just a few minutes.

When Liverpool made the emotional return to Hillsborough for the Barclays League game against Sheffield Wednesday, there were more than 32,000 people there, including 4,500 fans from Merseyside. But the Leppings Lane terraces were deserted, save for tributes which had been laid reverently on the steps. And the respective captains, Alan Hansen and Chris Turner, paid their respects by laying wreaths before the game began.

HILLSBOROUGH

Kenny Dalglish had asked that the occasion should be graced with dignity, and his appeal did not go unheeded. During the minute's silence which preceded the match, you could have heard a pin drop, and after the final whistle, the man in charge of the police operation, Chief Superintendent John Nesbit, summed up in a sincere and moving tribute: 'The Liverpool fans were a credit to their city, and to football generally. The game has been the winner tonight. I think all of us involved feel better, now that this occasion has taken place.'

DECEMBER

EIGHTIES END AS THEY BEGAN

Liverpool rounded off the 1980's by claiming the top spot in the First Division, just as they had done at the end of the 1970's, and in the last month of 1989 they were unbeaten through half a dozen League matches, with two outstanding performances against Manchester City and Chelsea – both these games were away from home.

Rush on song

Indeed, Liverpool's home form was in contrast to their sparkling away form, but they managed to hold bogey-club Manchester United to a draw at Anfield, despite the fact that United had the better of the game, and they scored victories over Sheffield Wednesday and Charlton Athletic.

But the five-star displays were reserved for Maine Road and Stamford Bridge. At Manchester, Ian Rush struck twice and Peter Beardsley and Steve McMahon scored to make it a resounding 4-1 success story; and at The Bridge, Chelsea were overwhelmed as Rush scored two more goals, with Beardsley, McMahon and Ray Houghton making it a final scoreline of 5-2.

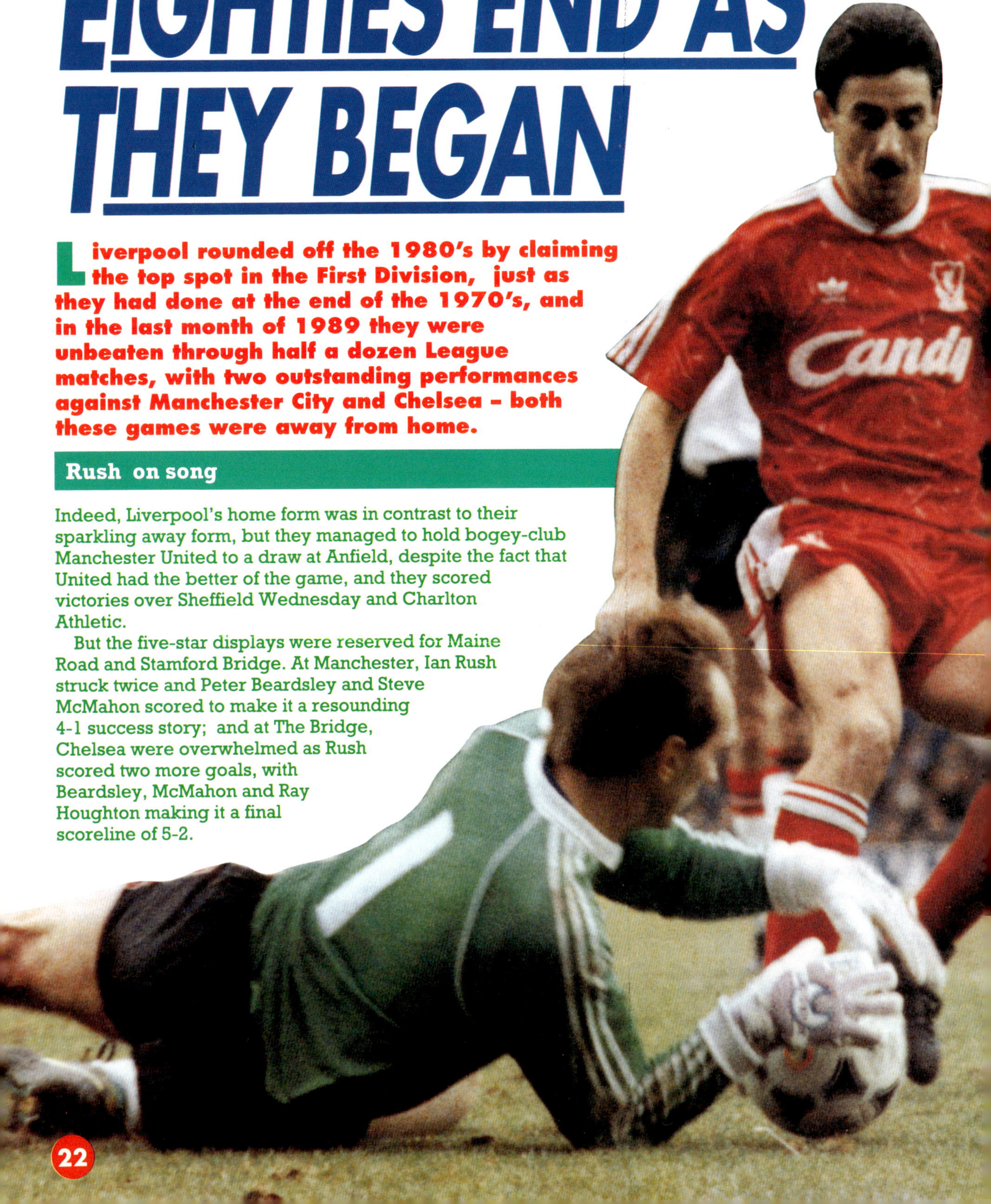

However, just to show that no-one could take anything for granted, the last League match of 1989 – against Charlton – saw Peter Beardsley and Steve McMahon sitting on the bench when the teams kicked off, though both got into the action as the game went by. Kenny Dalglish made it clear at the after-match inquest that, as ever, he chose the team which, on the day, he felt would do the job best for Liverpool. John Barnes, making a welcome return after injury, justified his selection by scoring the winner which put Liverpool four points ahead of second-placed Aston Villa and five in front of champions Arsenal.

RESULTS

Football League, 2 December

Manchester City 1	Liverpool 4
Clive Allen (penalty)	*Ian Rush* (2)
	Peter Beardsley
	Steve McMahon

Football League, 9 December

Liverpool 1	Aston Villa 1
Peter Beardsley	*Ian Olney*

Football League, 16 December

Chelsea 2	Liverpool 5
Gordon Durie	*Ian Rush* (2)
Kerry Dixon	*Peter Beardsley*
	Ray Houghton
	Steve McMahon

Football League, 23 December

Liverpool 0	Manchester United 0

Football League, 26 December

Liverpool 2	Sheffield Wednesday 1
Jan Molby	*Dalian Atkinson*
Ian Rush	

Football League, 30 December

Liverpool 1	Charlton Athletic 0
John Barnes	

League Position

	P.	W.	D.	L.	F.	A.	Pts.	Position
Liverpool	21	12	5	4	42	21	41	1st

Above: Ray Houghton gets past his marker as Liverpool beat Wednesday 2-1 on Boxing Day.

Bottom: Peter Beardsley loses Pallister and Blackmore, but the match with United finished goalless.

Far left: Ian Rush had never scored against Manchester United, and they were handing out no presents two days before Christmas at Anfield.

THE CLUB WITH T·H·R·E·E CAPTAINS

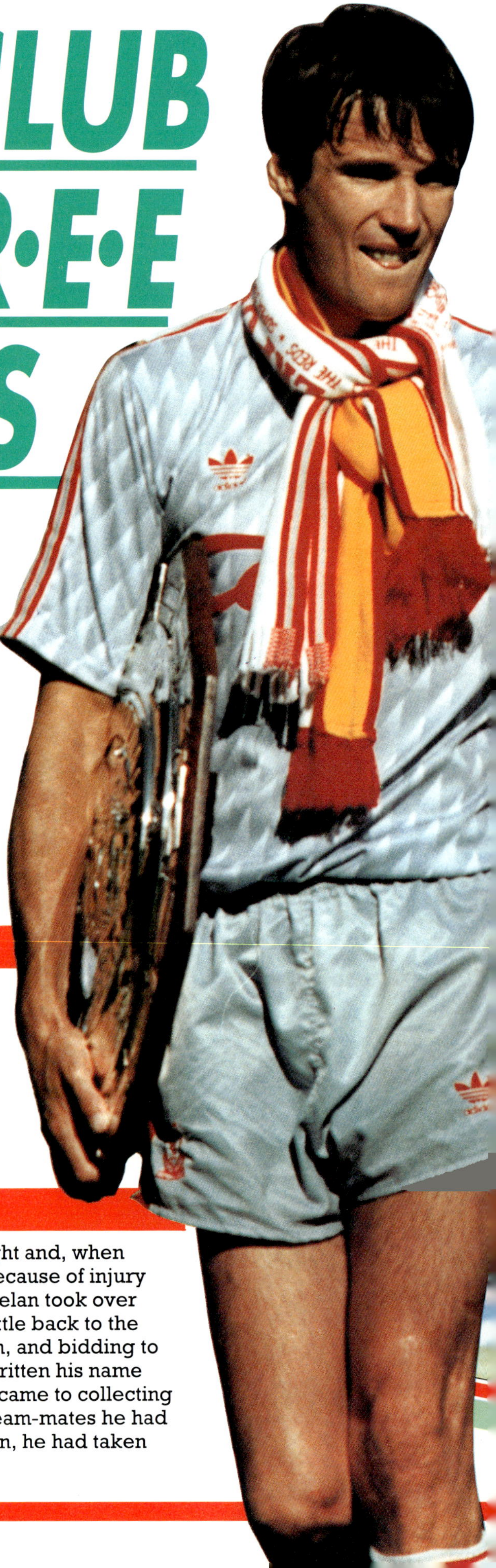

Ask your friends to name a club which has no fewer than THREE captains in its first team. . . and if they give the answer as Liverpool, then it shows that they really know their football.

At Liverpool, Alan Hansen, a Scotland international, is the team skipper on a regular basis; Republic of Ireland international Ronnie Whelan is the man who gets the job when Alan is absent; and – should both these men have to miss a match together – there's a third man who could step up to collect the captain's armband without turning a hair. Because Glenn Hysen is the captain of Sweden, and he led them to the finals of the 1990 World Cup in Italy.

Cup-winning captains

Remarkably, although Liverpool have won the FA Cup on only four occasions, both Alan Hansen and Ronnie Whelan have had the honour of going up the famous steps at Wembley to receive the trophy. And that could make them unique, because it's doubtful if there are two other first-team regulars at any club in Britain, or maybe even in Europe, who can claim to hold that distinction.

Record-breaker

Alan Hansen has never been one for hogging the limelight and, when he had to miss almost the whole of the 1988-89 season because of injury problems, he remained in the background as Ronnie Whelan took over the captaincy. For Alan, it was a long and often lonely battle back to the top but 1989-90 saw him kicking off in the first team again, and bidding to lead the club to more honours. Indeed, he had already written his name into the record books at Liverpool Football Club, when it came to collecting League championship medals because like two former team-mates he had won no fewer than seven. And by the end of the campaign, he had taken his tally to eight, thus matching the haul of Phil Neal.

The Liverpool skipper has also played more derby games against Everton than anyone else who has worn Liverpool's colours – he overtook Ian Callaghan's record of 31 appearances when Liverpool won 3-1 at Goodison Park early in season 1989-90. And he has topped the 600-game mark for Liverpool and totalled more than 700 appearances during his career.

Far left: **Alan Hansen, Liverpool's Scottish captain in the 1986 'double' winning year, at Wembley in 1989 with the Charity Shield under his arm after the defeat of Arsenal.**

Above: **Ronnie Whelan leads out Liverpool. He took over the captaincy during Alan Hansen's absence with injury.**

Left: **Glenn Hysen, the Swedish international captain and an inspiring leader.**

TEAM OF THE DECADE

Below: Bob Paisley with the European Cup, just one of the avalanche of honours heaped on Liverpool during his term as manager of the Anfield 'Mean Machine'.

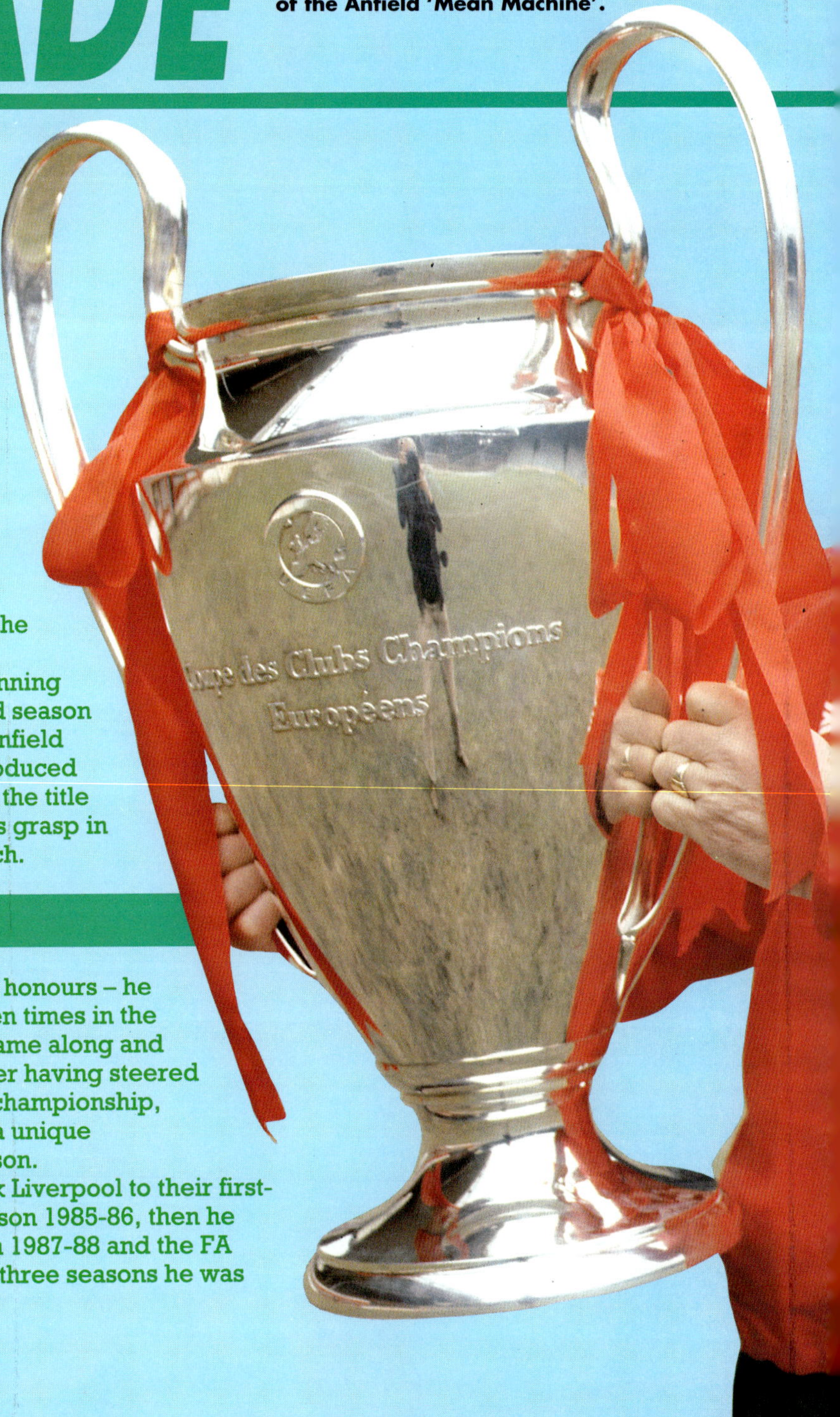

The team of the 80's? – Take a look at this list of trophies which Liverpool won . . .

They rounded off season 1979-80 by claiming the championship of the Football League – and then they really got down to business again! In season 1980-81 Liverpool won the European Cup and the Football League Cup; in season 1981-82 they carried off the League title and the League/Milk Cup; in season 1982-83, it was the League championship and the Milk Cup again; in season 1983-84 the championship trophy stayed at Anfield, along with the Milk Cup . . . and the European Cup was on the sideboard, as well.

Season 1985-86 saw Liverpool winning the League title and the FA Cup, and season 1987-88 took the championship to Anfield yet again, while season 1988-89 produced another success in the FA Cup, with the title prize being dashed from Liverpool's grasp in the dying seconds of their final match.

Managers of the decade

Bob Paisley's reign was strewn with honours – he was Manager of the Year half a dozen times in the space of eight seasons; Joe Fagan came along and was named Manager of the Year after having steered Liverpool to success in the League championship, the European Cup and Milk Cup – a unique achievement, and all in his first season.

Enter Kenny Dalglish, and he took Liverpool to their first-ever League-FA Cup double, in season 1985-86, then he settled for the League title in season 1987-88 and the FA Cup in season 1988-89. So, twice in three seasons he was named Manager of the Year.

Above: with 26 years of backroom service behind him and after only a season as team boss, Bob Paisley's successor, Joe Fagan, was named Manager of the Year in 1984.

More manager than player these days, Kenny Dalglish has taken over where Joe Fagan left off.

TEAM OF ALL STARS

How many clubs in the English League can claim that they could put out a first team composed entirely of fully-fledged internationals? – Very few, to say the least . . . but Liverpool can. And, for good measure, they could also field two international footballers as substitutes!

So how's this for a 4-4-2 line-up featuring an all-star selection?

Bruce Grobbelaar (Zimbabwe)

Gary Gillespie (Scotland)
Glenn Hysen (Sweden)
Alan Hansen (Scotland)
Steve Nicol (Scotland)

Ray Houghton (Republic of Ireland)
Steve McMahon (England)
Ronnie Whelan (Republic of Ireland)
John Barnes (England)

Peter Beardsley (England)
Ian Rush (Wales)

Substitutes: Jan Molby (Denmark), Steve Staunton (Republic of Ireland)

It's worth remembering, also, that when the World Cup finals were staged in Italy in the summer of 1990, no fewer than eight players from Liverpool were representing their respective countries.

Right: **with Liverpool since 1983, Scottish full-back Steve Nicol was Footballer of the Year for 1988/89.**

Left: Welsh-international Ian Rush left Anfield briefly, only to return and continue the success story.

Right: along with Whelan and Staunton, Ray Houghton completes a trio of Irish players at Liverpool.

Below: ace goalscorer John Barnes, an England cap in the Liverpool line-up.

FAREWELL TO 'ALDO'

An audience of more than 35,000 people saw John Aldridge bow out at Anfield, as Liverpool hammered nine goals past Crystal Palace. 'Aldo' – a scoring hero in FA Cup matches and a lifelong Liverpool fan – had agreed to join Spanish-club Real Sociedad, after it had become crystal-clear that Ian Rush, back from Italy, would be the No. 1 choice again at Anfield.

But as the goals flowed against Palace, John Aldridge got his chance to join in the scoring spree when he went on as substitute – and the timing was immaculate, because he scored with his first kick, since Liverpool had just been awarded a penalty. 'Aldo' spotted the ball, took aim and let fly . . . and that was another goal for Liverpool.

It was the 64th goal of his Anfield career, which spanned 104 appearances, and it was also the last he scored as he made his exit on what turned out to be an emotional night all round.

Adios Anfield

At the finale, as the Kop chanted his name, John Aldridge discarded his jersey and pulled off his boots, then threw them into the crowd, knowing that those fans lucky enough to catch them would treasure these mementoes as long as they lived. As for 'Aldo', he summed up: 'I wanted to leave those boots at Anfield, where they belong . . . I'll start with a new pair in Spain.'

He also admitted that 'there were moments when I came very close to brushing away a few tears. 'The team has been my life, but I realised I couldn't spend all my time sitting on the bench, and that's the reason I decided to move. But I don't think I would have moved to another English club, because I would have hated coming up against Liverpool. And when I finish my career, I'll be back with my son as a season-ticket holder. My heart will always be at Anfield.' The sentimental note was echoed again when John Aldridge was voted man of the match . . . a verdict with which no-one was prepared to argue, even if he hadn't been in the thick of the action for the full 90 minutes.

Right: **Having hurled his shirt and boots into the Kop, John Aldridge makes his way to the tunnel at the end of a distinguished career with the club he had supported as a lad.**

Below: **Fans and friends congratulate 'Aldo' after the game, in which he not only made his last appearance but scored his final goal for Liverpool – his 64th – before moving to Real Sociedad in Spain.**

PICK *of the* PIX

The best all-action pictures from another outstanding Liverpool season

Below: Swift on the turn, the 'Welsh wizard', Ian Rush, looks to have the beating of Spurs' skipper Gary Mabbutt.

Left: Gary Ablett demonstrates the 'hands-on' approach to work as he attempts to tackle scoring ace Gary Lineker.

Right: David Burrows intercepts a Rosario header in September's 0–0 meeting between Liverpool and Norwich at Anfield.

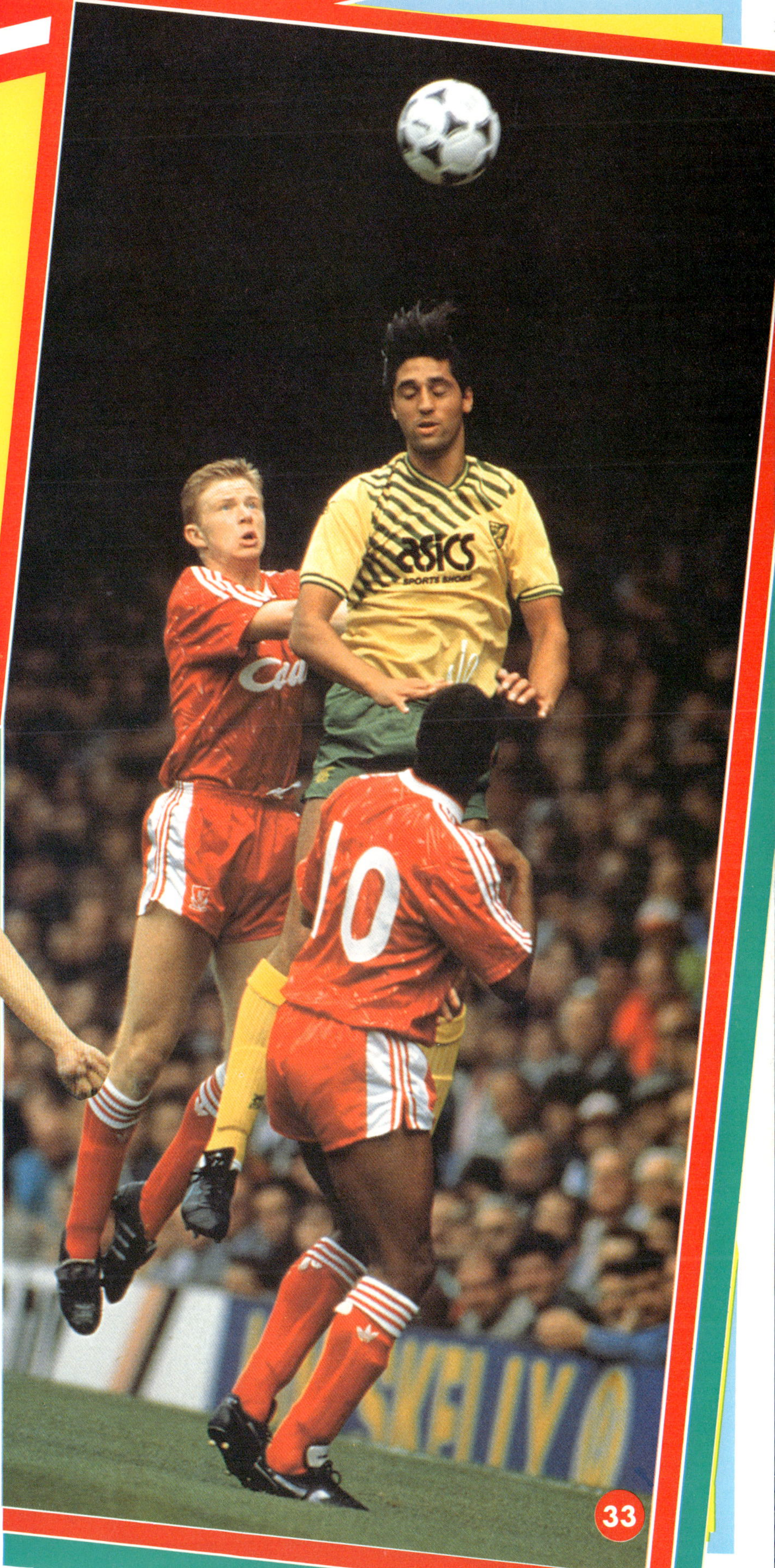

Left: Ronnie Whelan, in his time playing midfield, forward and full-back – you name it – here in his role as right-back during the goalless draw at Derby.

Right: Another prize picture from the eventful if goal-starved match with Norwich, as John Barnes leaps nimbly over prostrate defender Ian Butterworth.

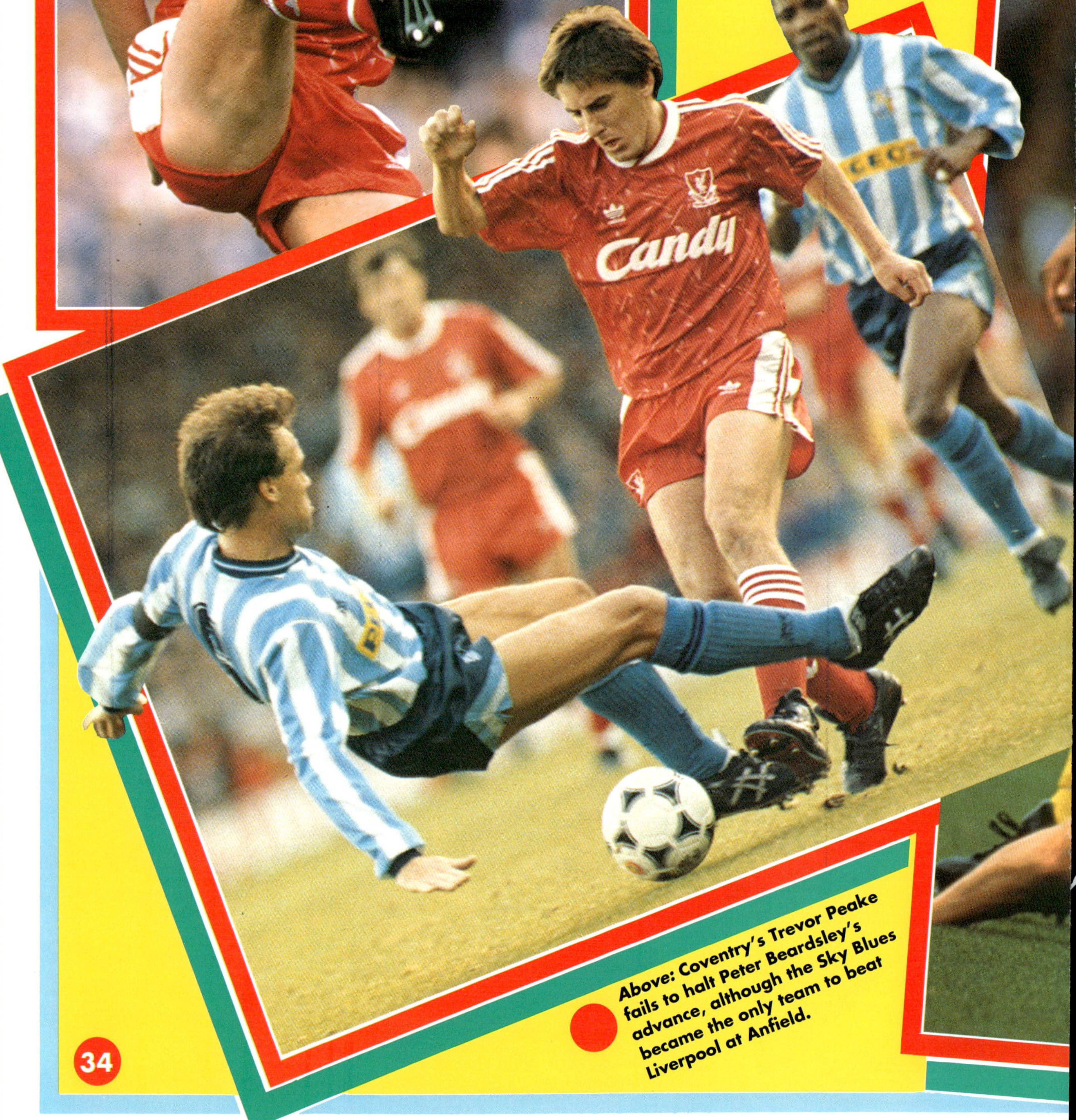

Above: Coventry's Trevor Peake fails to halt Peter Beardsley's advance, although the Sky Blues became the only team to beat Liverpool at Anfield.

PICK *of the* PIX

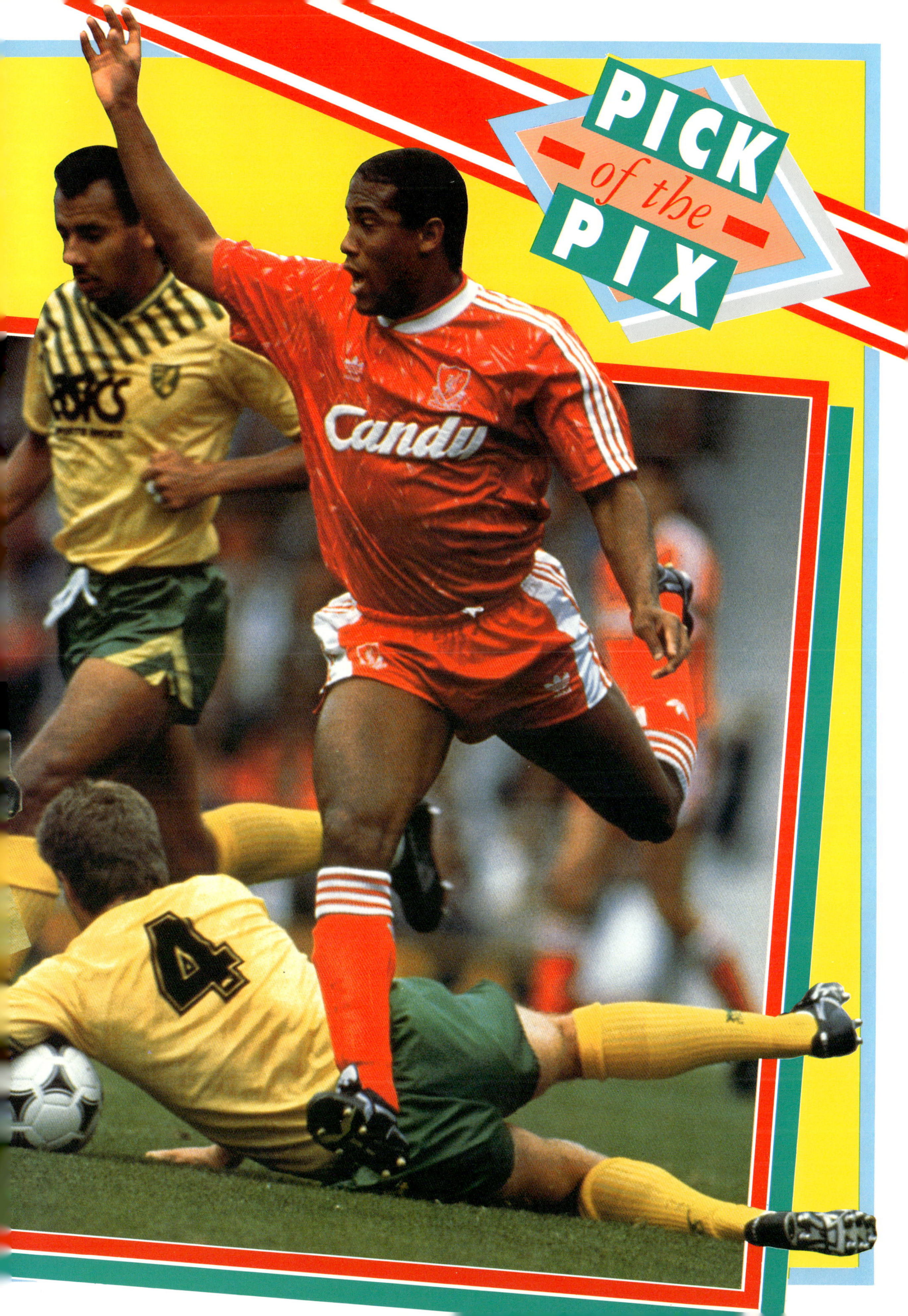

THE 28-YEAR HITCH!

The ace from Africa, Zimbabwe's Bruce Grobbelaar, one of the great characters of the game.

While many clubs change their goalkeeper once or twice every season, Liverpool have kept faith with their last line of defence to a staggering degree – in fact, through almost 30 years they have had only three recognised first-team 'keepers . . . and this means that others have stayed briefly, then been on their way.

The Big Three

The Big Three who made the No. 1 spot at Anfield their own have been . . . Scotland-international Tommy Lawrence; England-international Ray Clemence; and Zimbabwe-international Bruce Grobbelaar. And Ray Clemence had to wait two and a half years before he could oust Tommy Lawrence from the job!

Lawrence signed professional for Liverpool in 1957, finally broke through to the first team in season 1962-63, when he played 35 games in the League and the FA Cup. From then on, he was the No. 1 choice through the next seven seasons and took his tally of games to 387.

In six seasons, he missed only four matches, and in one season (1968-69) he set a record by conceding only 24 League goals in 42 games – a feat later emulated by Ray Clemence and then bettered.

Bargain basement buys!

Liverpool paid Scunthorpe just £15,000 for Clemence, and he stayed to total 656 games for them. After equalling that Tommy Lawrence record of having conceded only two dozen League goals in a 42-match season, 'Clem' improved upon the performance when, in season 1978-79, he conceded only 16 League goals! That was only one more goal than Preston North End had conceded in the League's first season (1888-89) . . . when they played no more than a score of games.

When Ray moved to Spurs in 1981 – he was still worth £300,000 then – Bruce Grobbelaar was pitched in at the deep end, after his £250,000 transfer from Vancouver Whitecaps . . . but he soon showed that, despite his touches of sheer showmanship, he could measure up to the job. From season 1981-82 he was ever-present until the end of the 1980s, and by the start of season 1990-91 he had taken his total of appearances for Liverpool very close to the 500 mark.

He has been a member of Liverpool's League-FA Cup double-winning side, claimed medals in the European Cup, the Milk Cup, and played in the world-club championships. And while Mike Hooper has made his presence felt in recent seasons, Brucie has managed to bounce back and remain the man in possession.

Above: **Ray Clemence was the Liverpool goalie of the '70s. His record-breaking run came to an end in 1981 when he moved to Spurs.**

Left: **The great Tommy Lawrence kept goal from the late '50s and through the '60s when Liverpool developed into the supreme side in League football.**

THE *John Barnes* FAN CLUB

The John Barnes Fan Club comes in all shapes and sizes, from star-struck youngsters to players and managers who have packed a wealth of experience into their own careers. And the impact of his dazzling skills has been made all the greater by the fact that, so often, he has produced a touch of magic in a game going out live on television.

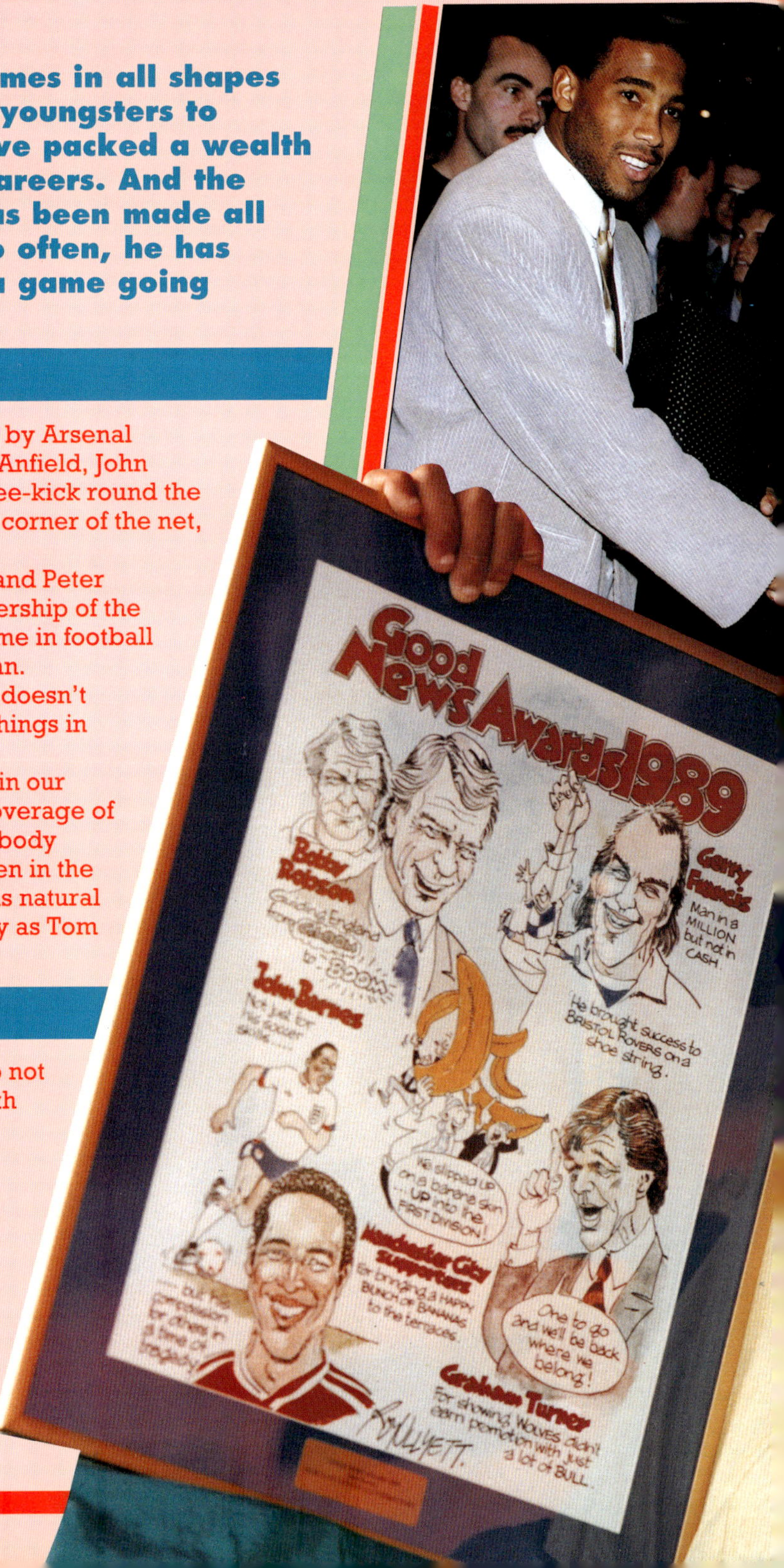

All-round player

For example, after having a penalty saved by Arsenal 'keeper John Lukic in the League game at Anfield, John Barnes had the last laugh as he curled a free-kick round the defensive wall and into the top right-hand corner of the net, leaving Lukic clawing at air.

Team-mates such as Bruce Grobbelaar and Peter Beardsley have been swift to claim membership of the John Barnes Fan Club, and another big name in football – Howard Kendall – is also a John Barnes fan. Nottingham Forest manager Brian Clough doesn't always see eye to eye with people about things in football, but says of Barnes:

'He has become the outstanding player in our league. His strength is phenomenal, his coverage of a pitch remarkable. I've never known anybody score the goals he does and appear so often in the left-back position. Marry those assets to his natural skills, and I'd put him in the same category as Tom Finney and Bobby Charlton.'

All-round man

Comparisons with Finney and Charlton do not stop at pure footballing ability either – both were noted for their sportsmanship and modesty – and so too is John. After the October Southampton game, a fan from Scunthorpe was moved to write: 'John Barnes – what a player! And what a sportsman! Following Liverpool's 4-1 defeat, John went into the home dressing-room and congratulated Saints' young players on their performance. Oh, that the game had more like John. Then the ugly side of football would soon disappear.'

Above: **John Barnes, who made himself instantly popular on his arrival at Anfield, and has been voted Footballer of the Year twice since he became a Liverpool player.**

Above left: **Man of the Match yet again! John Barnes receives a magnum of champagne from the man he most needs to impress, manager Kenny Dalglish.**

Left: **Good news for John Barnes when the *League Club Directory* made him an award for 'services to football' in 1989.**

THE OLD HANDS

What have they got in common?

What have they got in common? They're all dyed-in-the-wool Liverpool fans. There's Sir John W. Smith, former chairman of the club and a supporter of the team for more than half a century; Bob Paisley, who has given 50 years' service to Liverpool Football Club as player, trainer, physiotherapist, coach, assistant manager, manager and director; and Oliver Gray, who was just one day old when this picture was taken . . . so he surely qualifies as Liverpool's youngest-ever supporter.

Liverpool's former chairman, who was knighted in the New Year's honours list, is pictured making a boardroom presentation to Bob Paisley, and behind them are men who have also given the club years of service. From left to right it's vice-president Mr. Cecil Hill, and directors Mr. Jack Cross, Mr. Sidney Reakes and Mr. Sydney Moss.

As for Oliver Gray, he caused his proud father, Simon, one slight problem, as Simon explains: 'I missed the big clash between Liverpool and Arsenal at Anfield, because my wife was expecting our second child. So I had to make do with watching the game on TV.

'As you can see from the photograph, we had a lovely baby boy, and he's pictured at just one day old. Myself and friend Andrew White are Kop season-ticket holders, and we regularly make the 410-mile round trip to Anfield from King's Lynn, in Norfolk. We have been keen Liverpool fans for more than 20 years . . . and I'm sure it won't be long before our children are visiting Anfield, too.'

– AND THE NEW FACES!

Left: Bob Paisley (seated right) receives a handsome memento from another veteran Liverpool supporter, and fellow-director, Sir John Smith, to mark Bob's fifty year involvement with the club.

Above and right: Liverpool's supporters come in all ages and sizes. Surely the youngest ever is one-day-old Oliver Gray. Here we see him kitted out and dreaming of future glory in front of a packed Kop. Meanwhile, seven-year-old Maura McSorley from Glasgow clearly enjoyed her day as match mascot for Liverpool v Villa.

QUIZ

9 Which club did Liverpool beat when they won the Football League Cup for the first time?
10 Which club did Liverpool beat when they won the UEFA Cup for the first time?
11 Liverpool won the European Cup in season 1983-84 on a penalty shoot-out. Whom did they beat?
12 From which club did Bill Shankly join Liverpool, when he became the manager at Anfield?

PICTURE QUIZ QUESTIONS

1 This Liverpool shirt usually belongs to Ian Rush . . . but in his absence here it's being worn by someone else. Can you name the No. 9?
2 It's a goal! And the question is . . . can you name the man who scored it? – But don't be fooled by the No. 3 on his back!
3 Heads I win . . . and while John Barnes goes one way, who's the player looking in the opposite direction? – A clue . . . he's changed clubs since this game was played.
4 It's a face-to-face . . . but who do the faces belong to? – Identify the players, please.
5 Twice in a season, at least, they're on opposing sides, but at other times they're team-mates. So name the man who's challenging John Barnes for the ball.

1 No cheating . . . without looking at the Roll of Honour, how many times have Liverpool won the championship?
2 Still no cheating . . . in which years did they win the UEFA Cup?
3 Name the first Liverpool captain to go up and collect the FA Cup.
4 Bob Paisley never won an FA Cup medal, but he did claim an Amateur Cup-winner's medal . . . . with which famous non-League club?
5 Name the club Liverpool defeated when they won the European Cup for the first time.
6 Name two players who both won eight championship medals with Liverpool.
7 Name the six men who all wore Liverpool's colours, and who are now on the backroom staff at Anfield.
8 Which club did Liverpool beat when they won the FA Cup for the first time?

5

2

PICTURE QUIZ ANSWERS

1 Ray Houghton. 2. Barry Venison (No. 3), after having scored his first-ever goal for Liverpool. 3. Neil Webb, then of Nottingham Forest and now with Manchester United. 4. Steve McMahon (Liverpool) and Steve Hodge (Nottingham Forest). 5. Bryan Robson, captain of England and Manchester United.

QUIZ ANSWERS

1 Liverpool have won the championship 18 times.
2 Liverpool won the UEFA Cup in seasons 1972-73 and 1975-76.
3 Ron Yeats, when Liverpool won the FA Cup for the first time, in 1965.
4 Bob Paisley won an Amateur Cup medal with Bishop Auckland.
5 Liverpool defeated Borussia Moenchengladbach, to win the European Cup for the first time, in 1977.
6 Alan Hansen and Phil Neal.
7 The backroom men are Ronnie Moran, Roy Evans, Phil Thompson, Steve Heighway, Ron Yeats . . . . and, of course, team-manager Kenny Dalglish.
8 Liverpool beat Leeds United in the 1965 FA Cup final.
9 Liverpool beat West Ham United, to win the Football League Cup for the first time.
10 Liverpool beat Borussia Moenchengladbach, to win the UEFA Cup for the first time.
11 Liverpool beat AS Roma on a penalty shoot-out in the 1984 European Cup final.
12 Bill Shankly left Huddersfield Town, when he became Liverpool's manager.

3

WHAT THEY SAY

Liverpool took us apart. Their first four goals were one-to-ones. They knocked it about at the back, and you could hear the crowd jeering them for doing so . . . but, suddenly, they were in a scoring position.

Chelsea 'keeper Dave Beasant, after Liverpool's 5-2 victory at Stamford Bridge.

Liverpool's secret is that they all fight for the ball, then give it and then move. It's give-it-and-go, like the old Spurs' push-and-run. It's why they're the best team in the country, why they've been the most successful club over the past 30 years. When they're in that mood, they would have a helluva chance of winning the World Cup – and I do not jest. They're a well-oiled machine, with brilliant one-twos and clinical finishing. They pass to a red shirt, then move on somewhere else . . . Played properly, you can't get near them.

Chelsea manager Bobby Campbell – a Liverpool old boy – after seeing his side beaten 5-2 on home ground.

When Liverpool come at you, it's like being smothered by a blanket. They have so many players running off the ball. They give each other so many options.

Manchester City 'keeper Andy Dibble, after Liverpool's 4-1 win at Maine Road.

If I were given £12M to spend, I still couldn't guarantee being able to build a team capable of stopping Liverpool from taking the title. In recent years they've improved and refined the side, and have the best players around. Apart from the wages they can offer, they can virtually promise any prospective newcomer that he will win medals – and that's what motivates players as much as cash. Manchester United may be the glamour club of our Soccer, but Liverpool are in the business of playing and winning matches. Everything at Anfield is geared to the quality of the players put on to the pitch. They have never lost sight of the fact that they are a football club, first and foremost.

Aston Villa manager Graham Taylor.

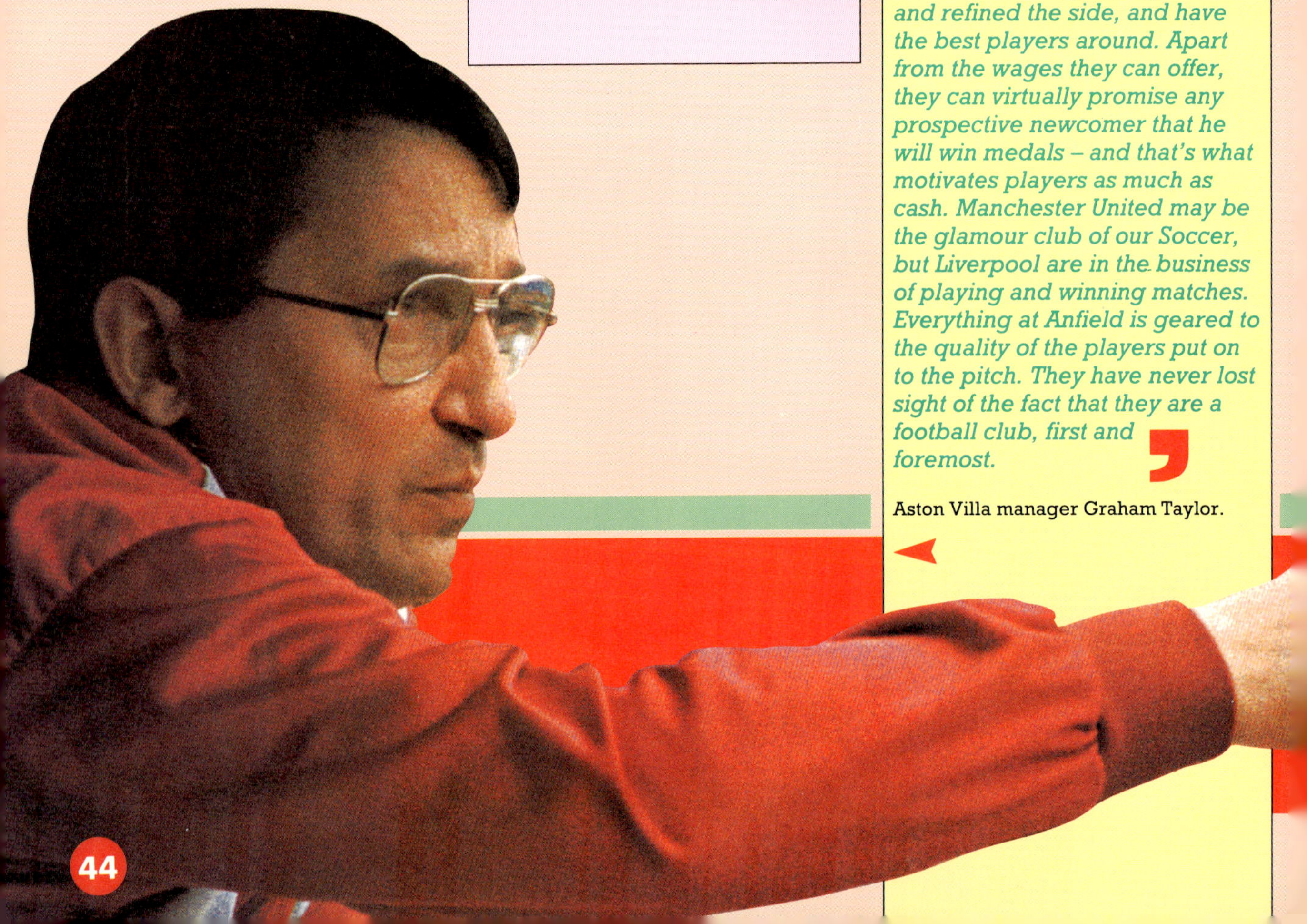

ABOUT LIVERPOOL

I didn't feel embarrassed, I didn't feel humiliated – I just felt numb, like my players. They came into the dressing-room as if they'd just gone 15 rounds with Mike Tyson. It was a proud moment for me, coming here as a manager . . . but I think this will haunt all of us at Palace for the rest of our lives. I don't think we'll ever forget it.

I couldn't believe what I was hearing from their dug-out when they were five goals in front. If we had been in their position, it would have been party time, but they were still demanding more effort and more concentration. If they'd had time for 15 goals, I'm sure they would have been just as demanding again.

Crystal Palace manager Steve Coppell, after seeing his side lose 9-0 at Anfield.

We did it at Liverpool last season because not only did we believe we could win there, but we desperately wanted to achieve it. But Liverpool have been doing it for 20 years with a great number of players and a variety of teams.

Arsenal manager George Graham, talking about talent – and the will to win.

JANUARY

Liverpool went through the first month of 1990 unbeaten, to make it 13 games without defeat, since the end of November, and along the way they set a new club record in the FA Cup, as they hammered Swansea City 8-0 in an Anfield replay.

Ian Rush celebrates the first goal in the 2-0 away win over Crystal Palace at Selhurst Park.

FULL SPEED AHEAD!

New Year Resolution

New Year's Day brought good news and bad news – a two-goal strike by Ian Rush against Nottingham Forest was followed by a two-goal comeback by Brian Clough's team. A third-round, 0-0 draw in the FA Cup at Swansea was followed by the 8-0 slaughter in the return, with Rush hitting the 12th hat-trick of his career and taking his tally of Cup goals for Liverpool to 26 in 29 outings, then Liverpool made amends for a 2-2 home draw against lowly Luton Town (Steve Nicol earned the point-saver) by going to Selhurst Park and clocking up a double over Crystal Palace. This time out, it wasn't 9-0, but 2-0 was good enough . . . then came two FA Cup-ties against Norwich, with Liverpool winning the Anfield replay, in which Peter Beardsley was outstanding. He made two goals, scored the third from the penalty spot.

Back in the groove

So, at the end of the month, Liverpool still topped the First Division table (on goal difference from Aston Villa) and they were through to the fifth round of the FA Cup. Apart from Ian Rush back on the goal standard – his haul was six in seven games – Peter Beardsley was back to top form, and he earned a special tribute from team-manager Kenny Dalglish after his sparkling performance in the replay against Norwich . . . the third game on the trot in which he had won star billing.

Steve Staunton in action at Anfield as Norwich go down 3-1 to the Reds in the FA Cup fourth-round replay.

RESULTS

Football League, 1 January

Nottingham Forest 2	Liverpool 2
Steve Hodge, Nigel Clough (penalty)	*Ian Rush* (2)

Football League, 13 January

Liverpool 2	Luton Town 2
John Barnes	*Kingsley Black*
Steve Nicol	*Kurt Nogan*

Football League, 20 January

Crystal Palace 0	Liverpool 2
	Ian Rush
	Peter Beardsley

FA Cup – third round, 6 January

Swansea City 0	Liverpool 0

FA Cup – third round replay, 9 January

Liverpool 8	Swansea City 0
Ian Rush (3)	
John Barnes (2)	
Peter Beardsley	
Ronnie Whelan	
Steve Nicol	

FA Cup – fourth round, 28 January

Norwich City 0	Liverpool 0

FA Cup – fourth round replay, 31 January

Liverpool 3	Norwich City 1
Steve Nicol	*Robert Fleck*
John Barnes	
Peter Beardsley (pen)	

League Position

	P.	W.	D.	L.	F.	A.	Pts.	Position
Liverpool	24	13	7	4	48	25	46	1st

DERBY-GAME DOUBLE!

Liverpool chalked up a derby-game double over Everton, scoring a nap hand of goals in all, while conceding two.

The Goodison duel looked like going in Everton's favour when their £1M new boy, Mike Newell, struck the first goal . . . but Liverpool rapped back with three goals of their own, and team-manager Kenny Dalglish summed up: 'This is probably as well as we have played in any derby game during the last few years.'

Liverpool's goals came as John Barnes soared to meet a cross from Peter Beardsley and steer a power-packed header past 'keeper Neville Southall; then it was the turn of Ian Rush. And, as one critic wrote: 'The spectre of Rush will haunt Everton fans for ever. Over the years, he has been their biggest heart-breaker. And he destroyed them yet again, with two glorious goals that give him an amazing 23 in 24 meetings between these deadly rivals.'

Rush didn't get his name on the scoresheet in the Anfield

Ian Rush, scourge of the Toffee Men once again, scored two of the three Liverpool goals in the first leg of the local derby games with neighbours Everton.

return – Neville Southall foiled him with a point-blank save – but Liverpool still won 2-1, with a goal from John Barnes after just 11 minutes and a Peter Beardsley spot-kick on the half-hour. In a first half dominated by Liverpool, Everton just managed to pull a goal back when there was merely a minute to go to half-time; but though they had the better of the second-half exchanges, the damage had been done. So it was six points out of six for Liverpool.

Just making sure! Ian Rush winds up with the ball and a defender in the net during an eager display that brought his derby-goal tally to 23 in 24 games against the old Merseyside enemy.

Below: **a cannonball header from John Barnes provided the equalizer and set Liverpool on the road to victory in the Goodison game.**

FEBRUARY

Liverpool went through February unbeaten – that made it a run of 16 matches without defeat, from November 29 – but lost their top-of-the-table spot to Aston Villa, though there were only two points in it, at the end of the month.

The elusive Peter Beardsley kept the Norwich defenders on their toes, but was unable to add to his 14-goal tally during the 0-0 draw with the Canaries at Carrow Road.

UNBEATEN AND ON COURSE

RESULTS

Football League, 3 February

Liverpool 2	Everton 1
John Barnes	*Graeme Sharp*
Peter Beardsley (penalty)	

Football League, 10 February

Norwich City 0	Liverpool 0

FA Cup – fifth round, 17 February

Liverpool 3	Southampton 0
Ian Rush	
Peter Beardsley	
Steve Nicol	

League Position

	P.	W.	D.	L.	F.	A.	Pts.	Position
Liverpool	26	14	8	4	50	26	50	2nd

Liverpool's first engagement was the return match against Everton, and at Anfield the Reds completed a double as they won 2-1, with goals from John Barnes and Peter Beardsley, who notched his second spot-kick goal in successive matches. Liverpool dominated the first half, but after Everton had made it 2-1 the contest became a different ball game, and it took a crucial save by Bruce Grobbelaar to ensure that Liverpool scored maximum points. The 'keeper tipped a Neil McDonald piledriver over the bar at a time when Everton were threatening to take command and even stage a winning comeback.

The next encounter was the Barclays League game at Norwich, and while there were no goals Liverpool were happy to come away with a point. Then they came up against Southampton – winners by four goals to one at The Dell in the League match – and the world of football waited to see if the Saints could come out on top again, in the FA Cup.

The Reds go marching on

They had Liverpool old boys Jimmy Case and Sammy Lee on duty, but at the end of the day it was Liverpool 3, Southampton 0, as Ian Rush, Peter Beardsley and Steve Nicol did the damage, and Case, Lee and Saints team-boss Chris Nicholl were left to sing Liverpool's praises. So the Reds were still on course for a double of League title and FA Cup. . . .

And when it came to goals, Liverpool had three players among the division's leading marksmen. They were Ian Rush (19 from 34 appearances), John Barnes (17 in 30 matches) and Peter Beardsley (15 in 34 games).

Below: **Master of the midfield, Steve McMahon takes off in an effort to evade Ratcliffe's challenge during the 2-1 win over Everton at Anfield.**

TITLE RACE HOTS UP

In the first League game of the month Liverpool defender Gary Gillespie scored the winner against Millwall. Then whilst Arsenal were losing against QPR next day, Aston Villa lost at Coventry.

A week later Villa were top, after beating Luton, while Arsenal drew at Maine Road and Liverpool met Rangers in the FA Cup.

A two-all draw was followed by a replay which Liverpool won by a goal from Beardsley, to leave them facing Crystal Palace in the semi finals.

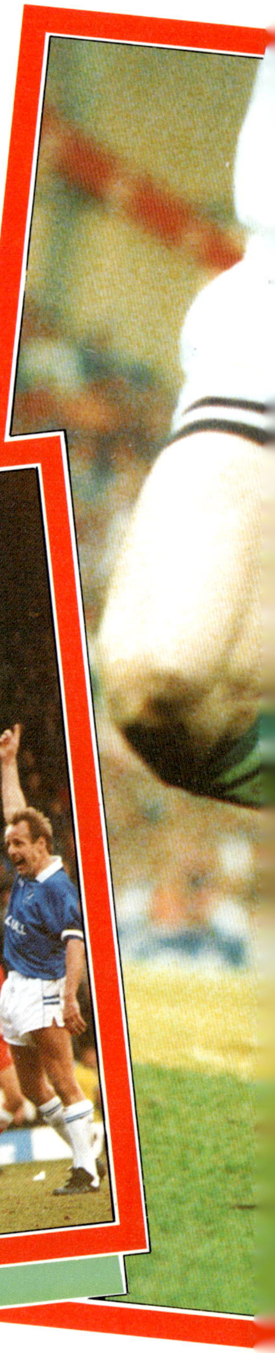

See-Saw Struggle

The following Saturday, Arsenal lost at home but Villa won at Derby, leaving Liverpool to face United at Old Trafford. Villa were five points clear, but Liverpool had two games in hand . . . and they won the Manchester duel thanks to two goals from John Barnes.

March 21, and things were warming up; Liverpool lost 1-0 at Spurs, Villa drew at Loftus Road, then lost against Palace; and Arsenal beat Derby. Then on the final Saturday, Liverpool regained pole position on goal difference.

As Arsenal beat Everton, Liverpool met Southampton, introducing substitute Ronny Rosenthal. Goals from Barnes and Rush ensured a 3-2 victory, and 24 hours later came Villa's home defeat by Manchester City.

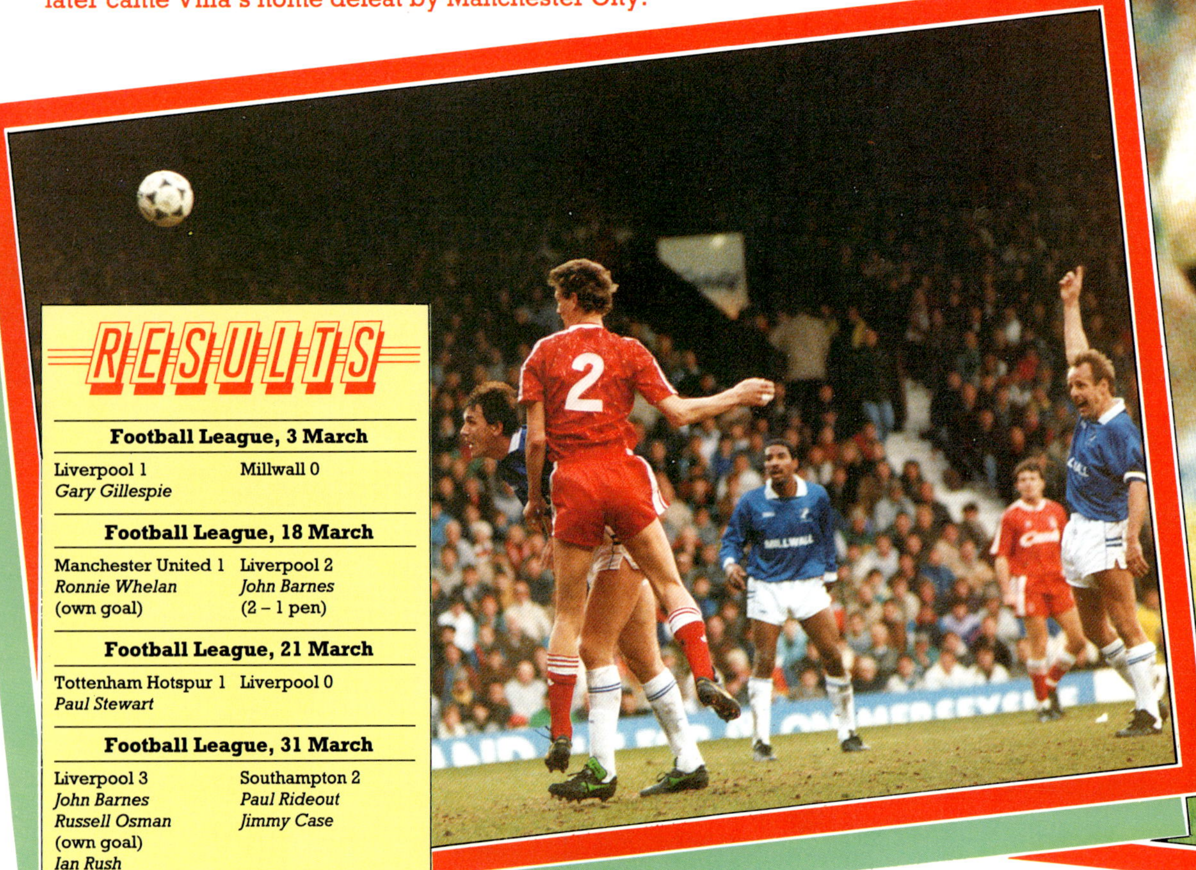

RESULTS

Football League, 3 March	
Liverpool 1 *Gary Gillespie*	Millwall 0
Football League, 18 March	
Manchester United 1 *Ronnie Whelan* (own goal)	Liverpool 2 *John Barnes* (2 – 1 pen)
Football League, 21 March	
Tottenham Hotspur 1 *Paul Stewart*	Liverpool 0
Football League, 31 March	
Liverpool 3 *John Barnes* *Russell Osman* (own goal) *Ian Rush*	Southampton 2 *Paul Rideout* *Jimmy Case*

MARCH

Below left: Anfield defender Gary Gillespie moves up front to set the seal on Liverpool's first victory of the month, a 1–0 home win over Millwall.

Below: At the end of the month, Ian Rush was one of the marksmen as the Reds beat Southampton 3–2 to take Liverpool one step closer to the Championship.

RESULTS

FA Cup – sixth round, 11 March

Queen's Park Rangers 2	Liverpool 2
Ray Wilkins	*John Barnes*
Simon Barker	*Ian Rush*

FA Cup – sixth round replay, 14 March

Liverpool 1	Queen's Park Rangers 0
Peter Beardsley	

League Position

	P.	W.	D.	L.	F.	A.	Pts.	Position
Liverpool	30	17	8	5	56	30	59	1st

Liverpool's defence of the FA Cup began at Swansea City's Vetch Field and ended at Villa Park, after extra time in a dramatic semi-final against Crystal Palace. In between, they broke a club record in the competition and played two matches in almost every round.

Early Battles

The third-round tie at Swansea ended in a scoreless draw, thanks mainly to the goalkeeping heroics of Lee Bracey, a 21-year-old who was to term this 'the greatest day of my life'. But in the Anfield return, Bracey was subjected to a bombardment which produced no fewer than eight goals for Liverpool . . . it was Swansea's heaviest defeat and Liverpool's biggest haul in the competition proper.

In the next round against Norwich City at Carrow Road, the game went to a replay after a 0-0 draw. In the return match at Anfield, Liverpool won 3-1, with goals from Steve Nicol, John Barnes and Peter Beardsley.

Southampton, who had beaten Liverpool 4-1 in their League game at The Dell, believed they could get a result in the FA Cup at Anfield, but after a 3-0 Red's victory they were singing Liverpool's praises. The marksmen: Rush, Beardsley and Nicol.

Target in Sight

Liverpool's trip to Loftus Road in the next round resulted in yet another replay afer Barker's late equaliser. At Anfield, however, Liverpool did manage to retain their lead – just – after an early Beardsley goal.

So it was into a semi-final against Crystal Palace at Villa Park, with Palace the definite under-dogs; and when Ian Rush struck in the first half, it seemed Liverpool were on their way to Wembley. But Rush was injured and left the fray, Palace equalised in the opening minutes of the second half, and

More FA Cup magic, as record-breaking striker Ian Rush opens the scoring in Liverpool's 3-0 fifth-round defeat of Southampton in February.

VETCH FIELD TO VILLA PARK

it became a ding-dong battle for supremacy.

Palace scored again, and Liverpool had their backs to the wall in this, their 22nd semi-final overall and their fifth in six seasons in the FA Cup. But the scales tilted Liverpool's way again as Steve McMahon drove in an equaliser, then John Barnes scored from the penalty spot, after Steve Staunton had been downed. Those goals had come in a matter of just one minute . . . and there was very little time to go.

Beaten but Unbowed

However, Palace produced a final flurry of attacking, and Andy Gray nodded an equaliser to force extra time, with the 90-minute scoreline 3-3. Palace were second-best during the first period of extra time, but they launched attacking forays after the turnaround . . . and after 109 minutes of play they struck the decisive goal.

It came from Alan Pardew, and it left Liverpool with virtually no time to recover. Remarkably, Liverpool had scored 14 goals against Palace during the season, having won 9-0 and 2-0 in the League. But this time out, despite three goals in the Cup, Liverpool finished second-best as Palace went to Wembley to meet Manchester United.

Happy New Year! The first Cup-tie of the new decade for Liverpool saw them complete a stunning, 8-0 slaughter of Swansea and Ronnie Whelan (left) was just one of the Merseyside marksmen.

For once, it wasn't a football match which drew thousands of people to Anfield . . . it was a pilgrimage of remembrance on the afternoon of Sunday, April 15, 1990. Easter Sunday, in fact, was the first anniversary of the Hillsborough Soccer disaster, which had claimed the lives of 95 fans as Liverpool met Nottingham Forest in the 1989 semi-final of the FA Cup.

That turned out to be an ill-fated affair which lasted no more than a few minutes, and just one year later, the tragedy was recalled with a simple, yet solemn ceremony at Anfield, where bereaved relatives were joined by thousands of people who wanted to pay their respects to the 95 victims.

The service was televised live to watching millions, and the ceremony was led by the Archbishop of Liverpool, the Most Reverend Derek Worlock, the Bishop of Liverpool, the Right Reverend David Sheppard, and the Moderator of the Merseyside Free Churches, Dr. John Newton.

The families of the Hillsborough victims will have a lasting reminder of their loved ones with the 'eternal flame' which was unveiled by Bill Shankly's widow, Nessie. All the names of those who died are on this permanent memorial, which is close to the famous Shankly Gates.

THE ANFIELD MEMORIAL SERVICE

The scene at Anfield on the first anniversary of the Hillsborough disaster . . . Easter Sunday, 1990. Thousands of fans joined in an emotional and moving memorial service.

Inset picture: Members of the Hillsborough Family Support Group release 95 red balloons – one for each victim – before the Anfield League game against Nottingham Forest.

Opposite page: People file past the "eternal flame" which now permanently marks the Hillsborough memorial, close by the famed Shankly Gates at Anfield.

April and May

THE LAST Saturday in April saw Liverpool clinching the championship of the Barclays League – their 18th success, overall – while on the first day of May they were celebrating again as skipper Alan Hansen was presented with the trophy, to make the whole thing official.

As Aston Villa were drawing 3-3 with Norwich City on April 28, Liverpool were beating Queen's Park Rangers at Anfield for the

It's been a long, hard slog, but now's the time to relax. Footballer-of-the-Year John Barnes (*above*) takes time out to get his feet up, after his title-clinching goal against Queen's Park Rangers, while the Liverpool squad captures the mood of the moment after having beaten Derby County and collected the championship silverware. *Left*, Kenny Dalglish claims his third Manager-of-the-Year trophy in five seasons.

second time during the season. The first victory, in March, had taken them into the semi-finals of the FA Cup; the second victory, which produced three points, ensured that the title trophy returned from Highbury.

It was Liverpool's seventh match of the month, and while they lost a dramatic Villa Park semi-final against Crystal Palace in extra time, in the League they amassed 14 points out of 18, as they stormed to the championship with two games to spare.

Goals from Gary Gillespie and Ian Rush saw off Wimbledon at Anfield, and straight after the FA Cup upset Liverpool went to Selhurst Park and demolished Charlton Athletic with a four-goal salvo. Israeli-international Ronny Rosenthal, bidding to make his on-loan move from Standard Liège a permanent transfer, was the man of the match as he hammered a hat-trick.

Liverpool let slip a two-goal lead against Nottingham Forest at Anfield, so they had to settle for a point, and they looked like losing a key game against Arsenal, at Highbury . . . until John Barnes salvaged a late equaliser. When Chelsea visited Anfield, intent upon avenging a 5-2 defeat at Stamford Bridge, they suffered yet again as Liverpool beat them 4-1.

Reds show their mettle

And so to the last match of the month, with Queen's Park Rangers providing the opposition. In fact, Rangers shook the Anfield faithful by taking the lead, but Liverpool had the men for the occasion in Ian Rush and John Barnes. Rush levelled the score, Barnes was the match-winner, and each man claimed his 25th goal of the season, as the championship trophy returned to Anfield.

CHAMPIONS!

Salute to the Fans

Three nights later, when Liverpool played their final home game, against Derby County, almost 38,000 fans welcomed the Liverpool players, and there was tumultuous applause when Kenny Dalglish went on to take part in the proceedings as one of the substitutes. After the 1-0 win, during the players' traditional salute to the fans, he threw his No. 14 jersey into the Kop . . . which provoked the question as to whether or not this was his farewell appearance as a player. Time alone, of course, will tell.

Double winners

Liverpool were champions twice over, during season 1989-90, because while the seniors regained the First Division title, the reserves claimed the championship of the Pontins League. Oddly enough, they did so just like the first team, by clinching it with two matches to spare. While Liverpool and Aston Villa made it a two-horse race in the League-title chase, Liverpool and Nottingham Forest fought it out in the Pontins League, with the Anfield men coming through to win the title on points, as they beat Bradford City at Anfield.

Sky Blue dessert!

Even then, Liverpool hadn't finished, because when they went to Highfield Road for their final match, they gave Coventry City a goal start, then hammered half a dozen past former Anfield man Steve Ogrizovic, to pay the Sky Blues back for having been the only team to win at Anfield during the season.

It was a victory which prompted Liverpool manager Kenny Dalglish to look back over the campaign and say: 'People can compare past seasons as much as they want, but we have been the best this season by nine points and, for me, the last championship is always the most satisfying.'

Liverpool's six-goal feat at Highfield Road was all the more remarkable because, while they had a strong side out, their absentees included skipper Alan Hansen, Steve Nicol, Peter Beardsley, Ronnie Whelan and David Burrows. That win meant Liverpool had finished the season on a high note, as they totalled 79 points against the 70 collected by runners-up Aston Villa.

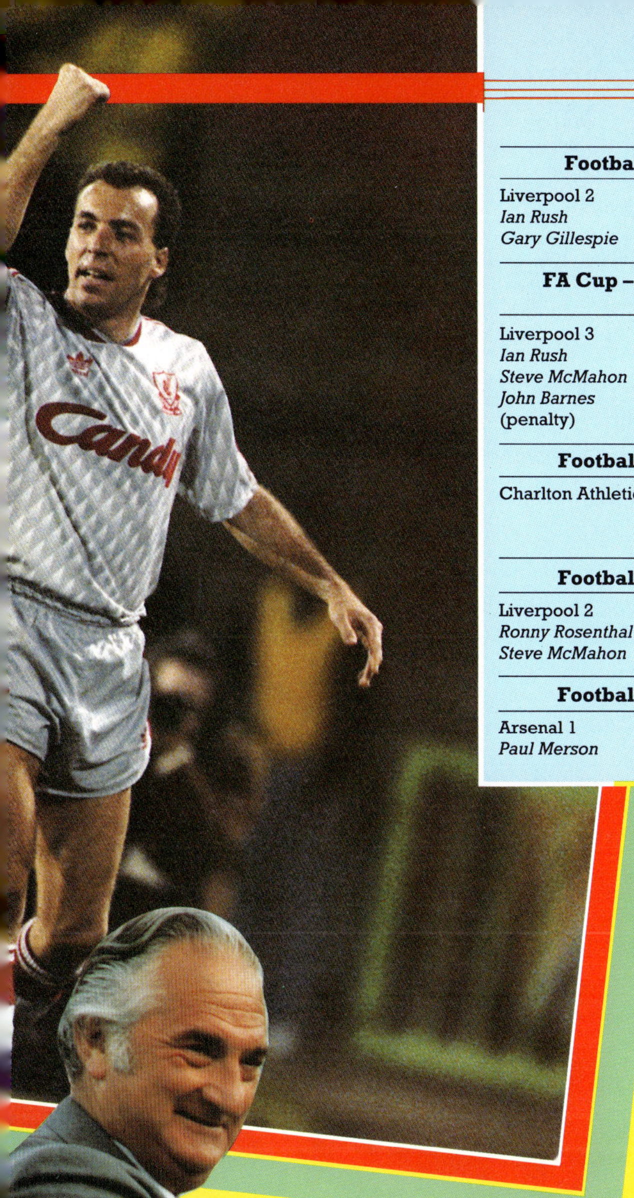

RESULTS

Football League, 3 April

Liverpool 2	Wimbledon 1
Ian Rush	*Alan Hansen*
Gary Gillespie	(own goal)

FA Cup – semi-final, 8 April, Villa Park

Liverpool 3	Crystal Palace 4
Ian Rush	*Mark Bright*
Steve McMahon	*Gary O'Reilly*
John Barnes	*Andy Gray*
(penalty)	*Alan Pardew*

Football League, 11 April

Charlton Athletic 0	Liverpool 4
	Ronny Rosenthal (3)
	John Barnes

Football League, 14 April

Liverpool 2	Nottingham Forest 2
Ronny Rosenthal	*Steve Hodge*
Steve McMahon	*Nigel Jemson*

Football League, 18 April

Arsenal 1	Liverpool 1
Paul Merson	*John Barnes*

Football League, 21 April

Liverpool 4	Chelsea 1
Steve Nicol (2)	*Kerry Dixon*
Ian Rush	
Ronny Rosenthal	

Football League, 28 April

Liverpool 2	Queen's Park Rangers 1
Ian Rush	*Roy Wegerle*
John Barnes (penalty)	

Football League, 1 May

Liverpool 1	Derby County 0
Gary Gillespie	

Football League, 5 May

Coventry City 1	Liverpool 6
Kevin Gallacher	*John Barnes* (3)
	Ronny Rosenthal (2)
	Ian Rush

Final League Position

	P.	W.	D.	L.	F.	A.	Pts.	Position
Liverpool	38	23	10	5	78	37	79	1st

Liverpool finished as champions.

Left: **Ronny Rosenthal . . . Seven goals in eight League games while on loan from Standard Liège clinched a transfer to Liverpool for the Israeli international, in a reported £1M package deal. (*Far left*) Liverpool's players salute the fans after the trophy presentations had been made when they played Derby County.**

It's trophy time . . . and Sir John W. Smith receives the £100,000 cheque which goes with the Barclays League title that Liverpool won.

ROLL OF HONOUR

Football League champions

1900-01
1905-06
1921-22
1922-23
1946-47
1963-64
1965-66
1972-73
1975-76
1976-77
1978-79
1979-80
1981-82
1982-83
1983-84
1985-86
1987-88
1989-90

FA Cup winners

1964-65
1973-74
1985-86
1988-89

European Cup winners

1976-77
1977-78
1980-81
1983-84

UEFA Cup winners

1972-73
1975-76

League/Milk Cup winners

1980-81
1981-82
1982-83
1983-84